MATH MAZES

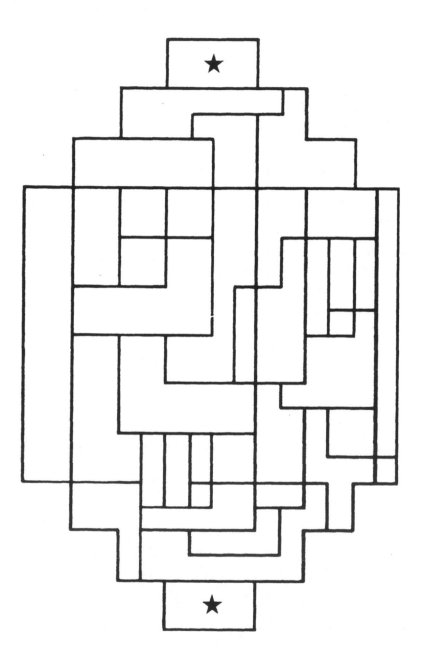

Carolyn Anderson

J. Weston Walch, Publisher

Portland, Maine

1   2   3   4   5   6   7   8   9   10

ISBN 0–8251–2315–1
Copyright © 1993
J. Weston Walch, Publisher
P.O. Box 658 • Portland, Maine 04104-0658
Printed in the United States of America

Contents

---

* Easier mazes (approximately 15 minutes or less)

Introduction

This set was formulated to be a tool to effectively promote reasoning and problem-solving skills within the classroom. With this material, students are forced to look at math in another light. Trying, testing, reasoning, and rethinking become part of skill development.

Educators are changing their focus from memorization and drill to adaptability, flexibility, and analysis. This focus will carry students to an even higher level of learning.

In utilizing this set, students are given a problem (maze) to solve. Typically in the past, students were asked to add up 25¢ + 35¢ + 40¢—a rote drill activity with minimal thinking involved. But by giving students a maze requiring collection of a specific sum, they are forced to analyze, reason, and use number sense to complete the task.

This set has:

- one sheet of self-contained activities that promote reasoning and problem-solving development
- material correlated with topics (for example, decimals—decimal maze) found in textbooks
- application with remedial to advanced students
- the advantage of being quickly available for a specific time, extra time, as openers, for enrichment, contests, problems of the day, etc.

Advanced students enjoy the challenge of these mazes. However, remedial students may become frustrated. To continue their interest and lead remedial students to a successful outcome, it may become necessary to give them helpful hints or show them the start to a correct path.

This resource is a must. Education is incomplete if drill is the only learning tool used. Teaching students to analyze, reason, and solve problems is a desirable goal of education.

Suggested Answers

1. "50" Maze

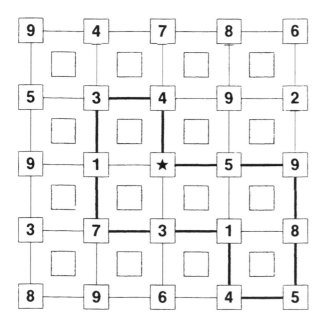

3. Circle Maze

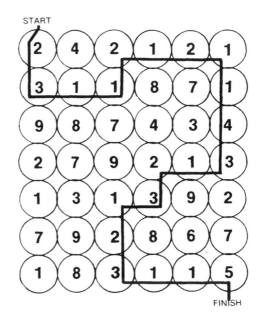

2. Even and Odd Maze

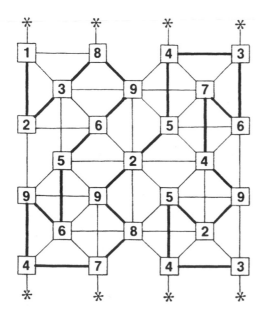

4. Counting Maze

START

5	2	3	1	1	1	2	3	2	1
3	2	2	4	2	3	4	4	2	3
4	3	4	3	5	1	2	5	1	2
4	5	5	1	2	4	1	4	5	3
5	1	2	3	4	5	2	2	3	4
3	5	4	5	3	3	4	1	1	5
5	4	3	2	4	5	4	2	5	1
1	4	5	2	1	2	3	3	3	2
5	1	1	2	5	4	4	5	4	3
4	2	3	3	5	2	5	2	1	2
3	1	3	2	1	3	4	3	3	1
5	4	3	1	3	5	5	2	5	2

FINISH

5. Shape Maze

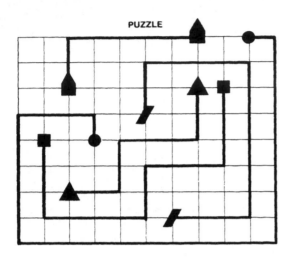

7. On Target Maze

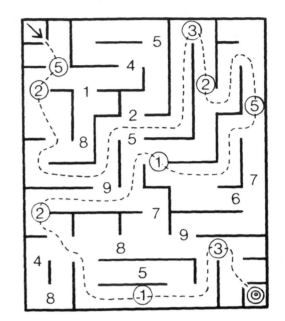

6. Route 55 Maze

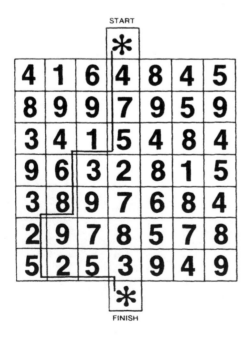

8. One-Way Maze

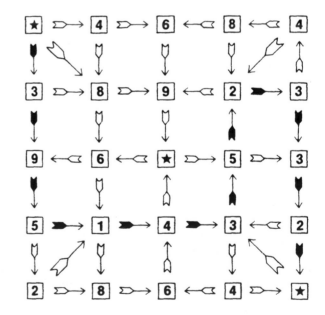

9. Math Symbol Maze

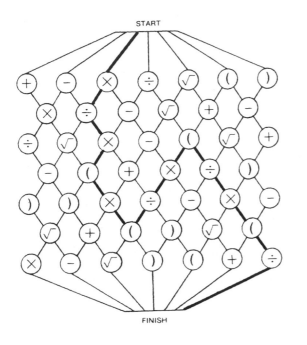

11. Area Maze

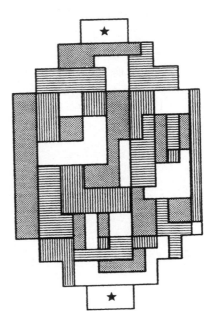

10. Optical Maze

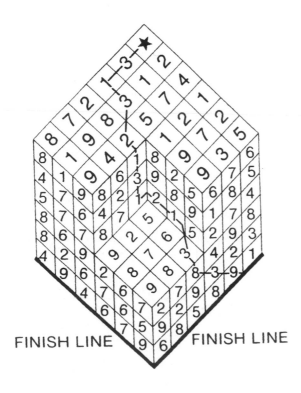

12. Highway Maze

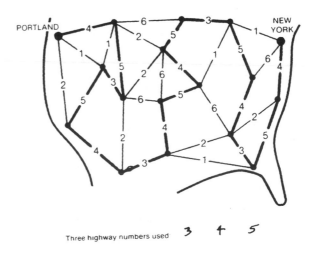

Three highway numbers used   3   4   5

13. Kriss-Kross Number Maze

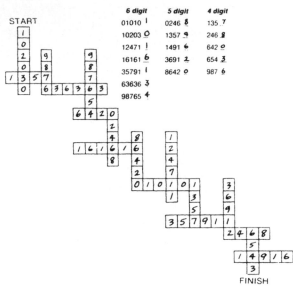

	6 digit		5 digit		4 digit
	01010	1	0246	8	135 7
	10203	0	1357	9	246 8
	12471	1	1491	6	642 0
	16161	6	3691	2	654 3
	35791	1	8642	0	987 6
	63636	3			
	98765	4			

15. Toll Road Maze

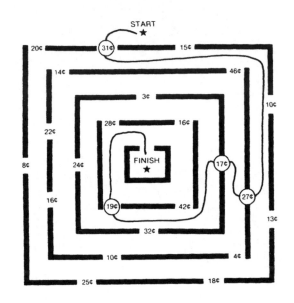

14. "Total" Maze

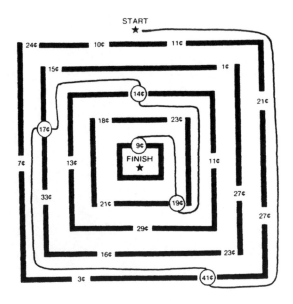

16. 50¢ Maze

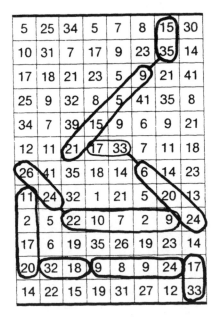

17. Path Maze

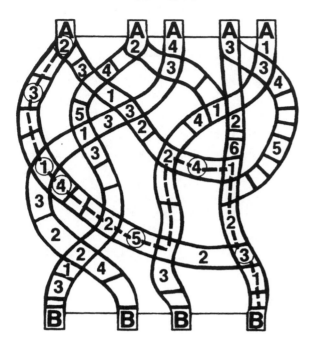

19. Collection Maze #1

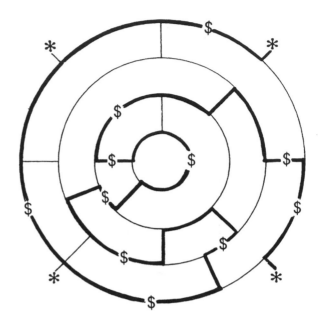

18. Bingo Maze

a. $34 \times 56 - 18 = 1886$
b. $512 + 349 - 146 = 715$
c. $2076 - 192 - 923 = 961$
d. $1715 \div 35 + 247 = 296$
e. $39 + 294 + 728 = 1061$
f. $63 \times 27 - 235 = 1466$
g. $22 \times 9 \times 24 = 4752$
h. $288 \div 12 + 211 = \mathbf{235}$

i. $215 + 49 + 62 = 326$
j. $1000 - 210 - 69 = 721$
k. $144 \times 12 \div 36 = 48$
l. $6 \times 8 \times 3 \times 8 = 1152$
m. $12 \times 12 \times 12 = \mathbf{1728}$
n. $24 + 327 = 351$
o. $29{,}163 - 28{,}728 = 435$
p. $38 \times 19 = 722$

q. $2050 \div 25 = 82$
r. $2050 - 1902 + 24 = \mathbf{172}$
s. $214 + 823 - 661 = 376$
t. $35{,}650 \div 31 \div 25 = 46$
u. $326 + 295 = \mathbf{621}$
v. $1 \times 2 \times 3 \times 4 \times 5 \times 6 = 720$
w. $1301 - 499 - 106 = \mathbf{696}$
x. $214 + 562 - 129 = 647$

B I N G O

2146	326	351	621	722
721	2066	222	235	3095
4752	561	FREE	1728	46
191	715	529	172	1206
245	1886	826	696	376

Five problems that made a BINGO: __h__ __m__ __r__ __u__ __w__

20. Collection Maze #2

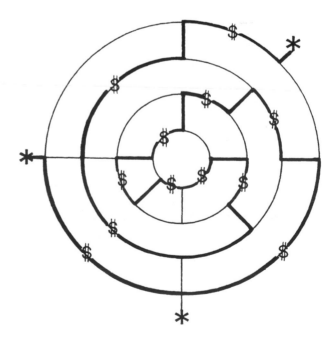

21. Fraction Maze

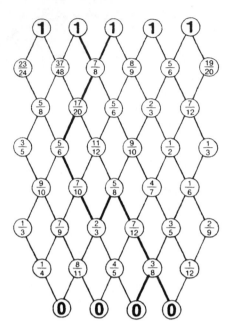

22. "Perfect Fit" Maze

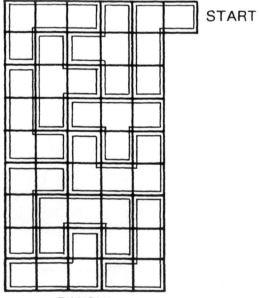

START

FINISH

23. Dollar Maze

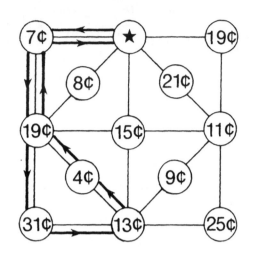

24. Magic Square Maze

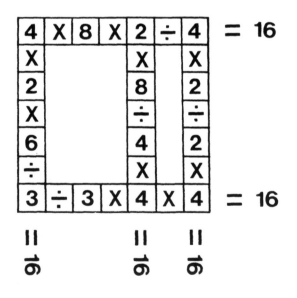

"50" Maze

Starting and ending at the star, move along any line in such a way that you accumulate a total of 50. (Note: you may not cut diagonally across squares or use a path more than once.)

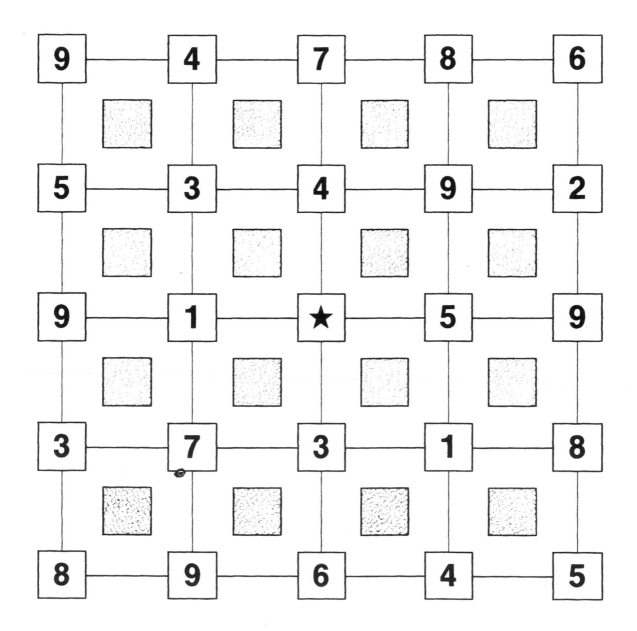

Even and Odd Maze

Begin at a star, pass through all the numbers, and finish at a star. The path you choose must alternate between odd and even or even and odd numbers (e.g., 3–2–7–6, etc., or 4–3–6–7, etc.). No path or number can be used more than once.

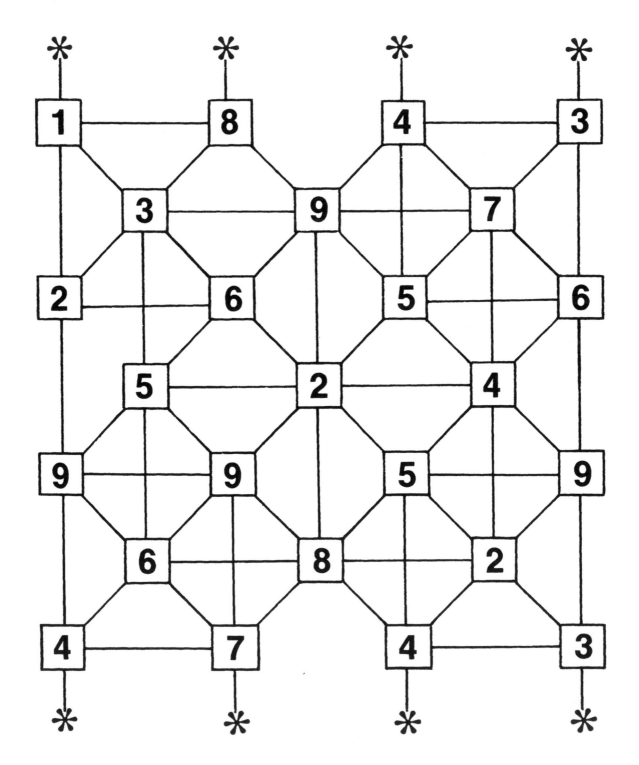

Circle Maze

Start at the indicated 2 on the top row and move to the 5 on the bottom row.
Find a path whose sum is 40. You may only move horizontally or vertically and
advance to a circle touching the previous circle.

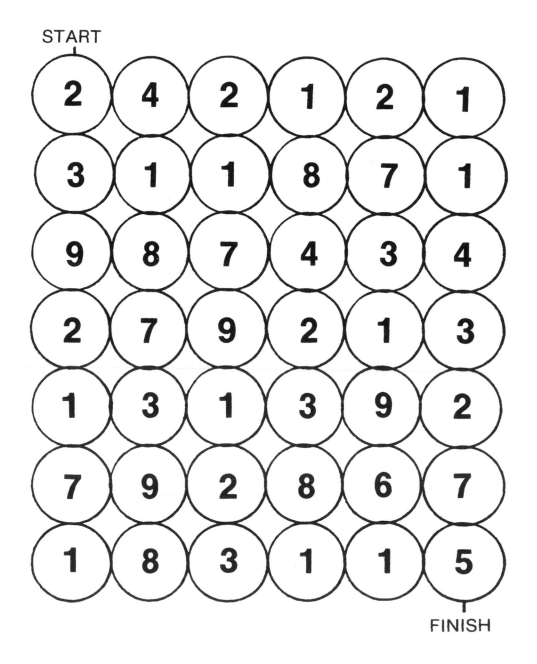

Counting Maze

Move from the top row to the bottom, so that the sequence 1 to 5 is repeated four times (1–2–3–4–5–1–2–3–4–5–1–2–3–4–5–1–2–3–4–5). Horizontal, vertical, or diagonal moves are allowed, but no number may be used more than once.

START

5	2	3	1	1	1	2	3	2	1
3	2	2	4	2	3	4	4	2	3
4	3	4	3	5	1	2	5	1	2
4	5	5	1	2	4	1	4	5	3
5	1	2	3	4	5	2	2	3	4
3	5	4	5	3	3	4	1	1	5
5	4	3	2	4	5	4	2	5	1
1	4	5	2	1	2	3	3	3	2
5	1	1	2	5	4	4	5	4	3
4	2	3	3	5	2	5	2	1	2
3	1	3	2	1	3	4	3	3	1
5	4	3	1	3	5	5	2	5	2

FINISH

Shape Maze

Find a path along the lines connecting one circle to the other circle, one triangle to the other triangle, one square to the other square, etc. No paths may cross or touch each other—not even at one point!

Examples:

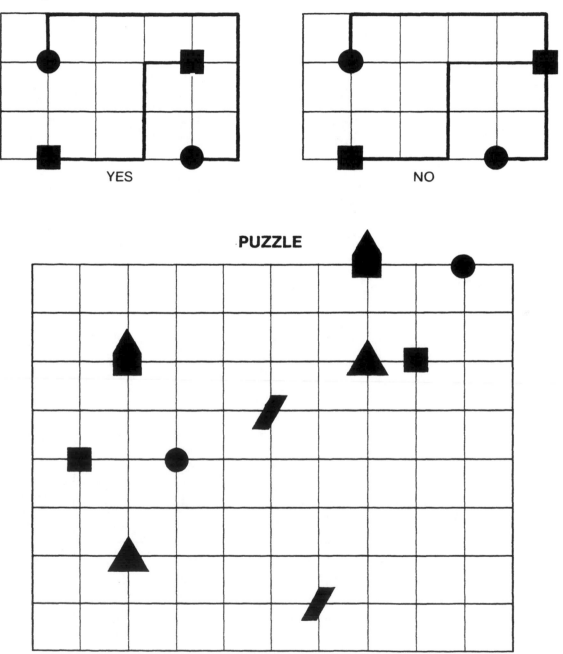

Route 55 Maze

Move from the start to the finish, collecting a total of 55. All moves must be either horizontal or vertical; no square can be used more than once.

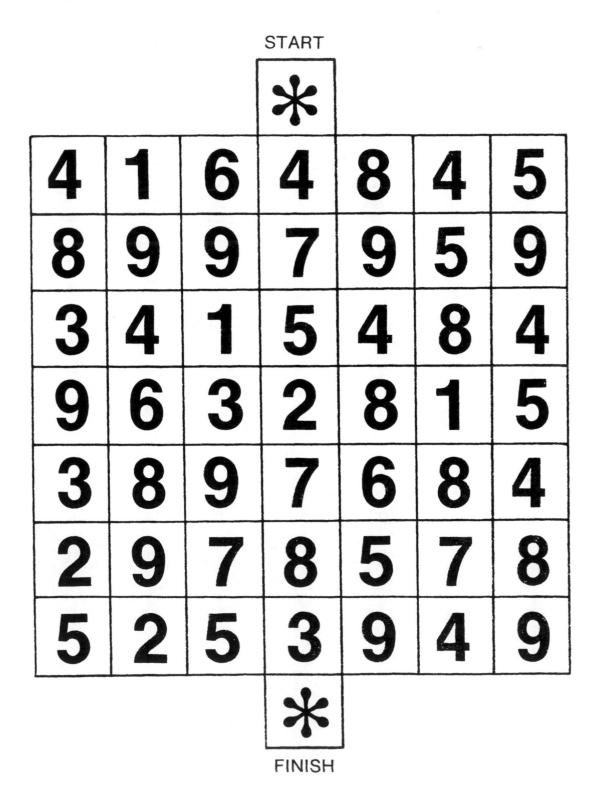

On Target Maze

Move through the maze from the arrow to the target with a path sum of 24.

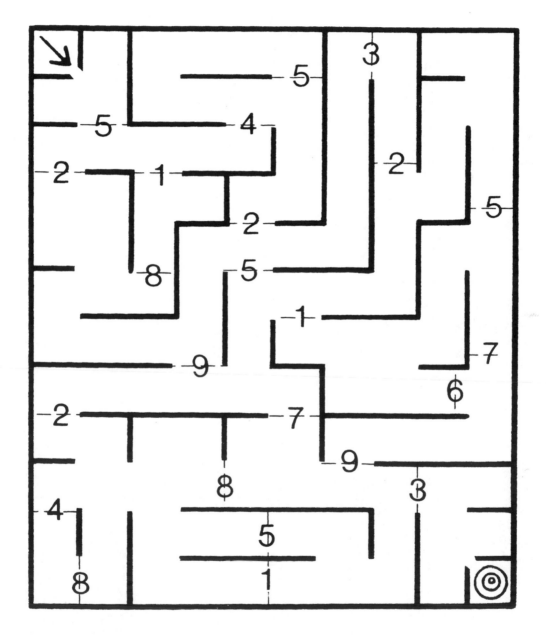

One-Way Maze

Find a path from any one star to another, moving in the marked direction with a path sum of 40.

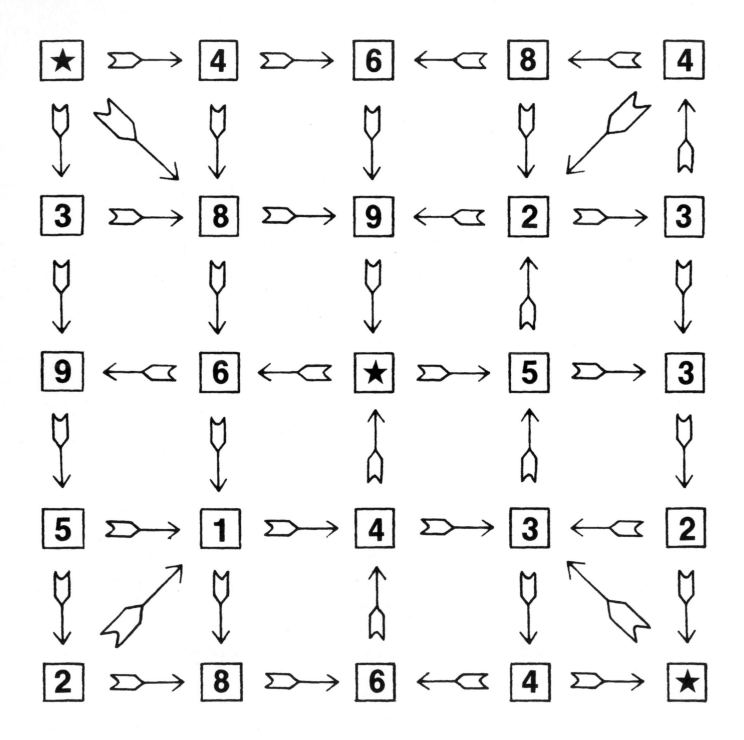

Math Symbol Maze

Pick any three of the seven symbols shown in the first row. Move from the start to the finish line only through circles with one of those three symbols in them.

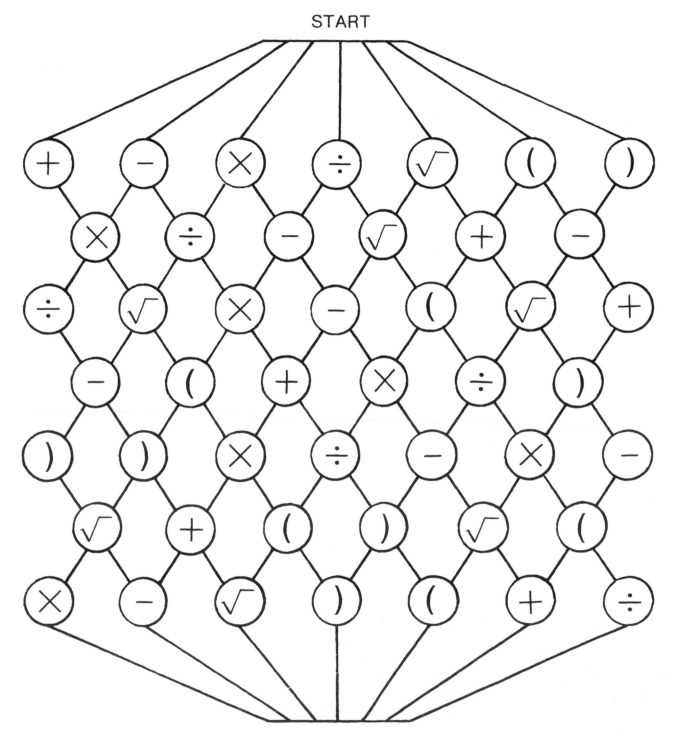

START

FINISH

Optical Maze

Find the path that goes from the star at the top to the finish line at the bottom with a path total of 40. Only moves to touching boxes (side or corner) are allowed.

FINISH LINE   FINISH LINE

Area Maze

Color the areas below from star to star in one of four ways.

leave clear: [   ]   shade in: [▓]   horizontal lines: [≡]   vertical lines: [|||||]

Color all the areas in such a way that areas that touch are not colored in using the same method (e.g., clear can't touch clear, shaded in can't touch shaded in, etc.). Even when four areas meet at a point, they must all be colored in differently.

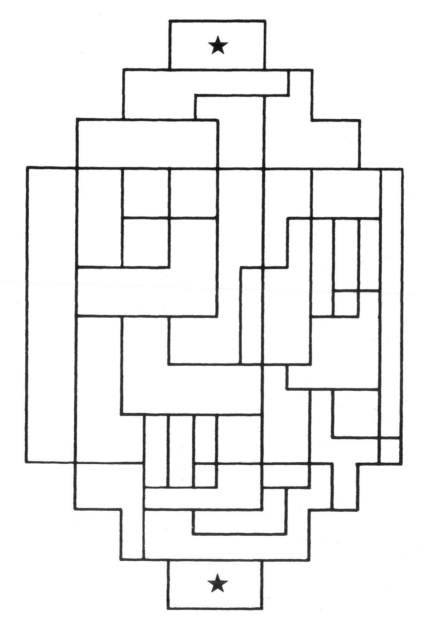

Highway Maze

Find a path from New York to Portland that travels through all the other towns marked. You must select three highway numbers (out of a possible six) and only use their marked paths. Remember to go to each town—but only once!

Three highway numbers used: _____ _____ _____

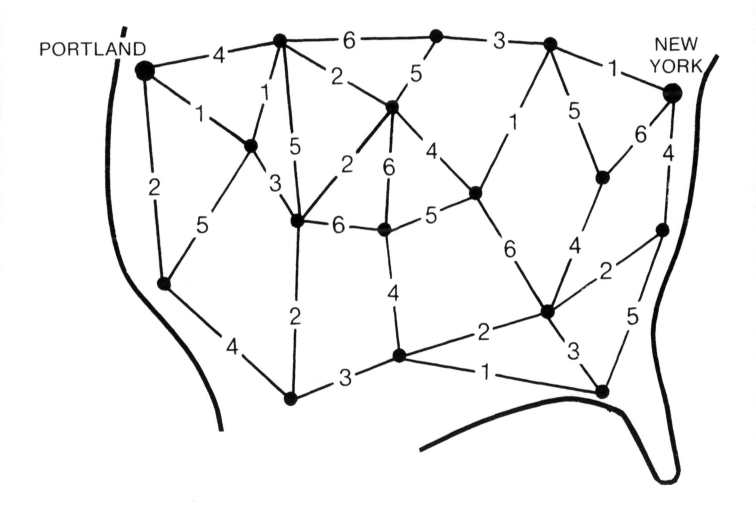

Name _____ Date _____

Kriss-Kross Number Maze

Determine the pattern and complete each of the 17 numbers listed below. Place the complete numbers in the maze using each one only once.

6 digit	**5 digit**	**4 digit**
01010 ___	0246 ___	135 ___
10203 ___	1357 ___	246 ___
12471 ___	1491 ___	642 ___
16161 ___	3691 ___	654 ___
35791 ___	8642 ___	987 ___
63636 ___		
98765 ___		

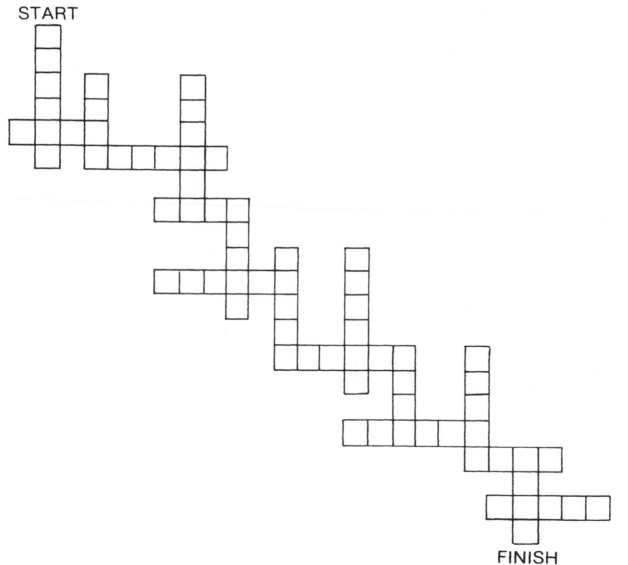

START

FINISH

"Total" Maze

Move from the start star to the finish star so that the sum of all the openings passed through equals $1.

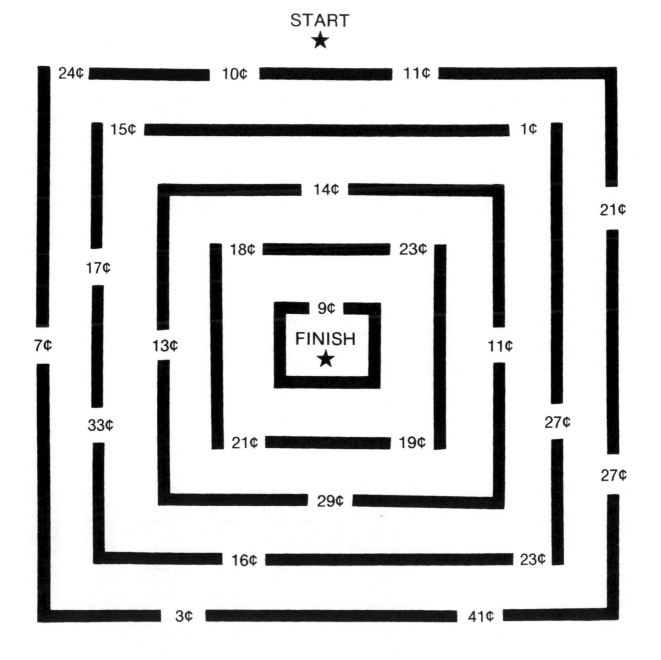

Toll Road Maze

Begin at the star marked "START" with $1. Move from that star to the finish star subtracting the amount of each toll road entrance from the dollar. End at the finish star with exactly 6¢ left.

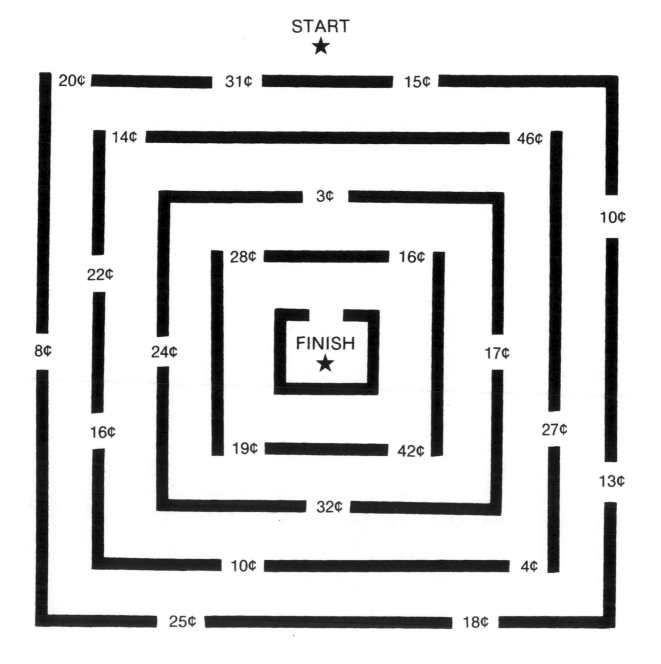

50¢ Maze

Circle groups of numbers adding up to 50¢ (see example). They will be found in a straight line, horizontally, vertically, or diagonally. They must touch. If all are correctly located, they will form a path from the top to the bottom line.

5	25	34	5	7	8	15	30
10	31	7	17	9	23	35	14
17	18	21	23	5	9	21	41
25	9	32	8	5	41	35	8
34	7	39	15	9	6	9	21
12	11	21	(17	33)	7	11	18
26	41	35	18	14	6	14	23
11	24	32	1	21	5	20	13
2	5	22	10	7	2	9	24
17	6	19	35	26	19	23	14
20	32	18	9	8	9	24	17
14	22	15	19	31	27	12	33

Path Maze

Find a path from any *A* to any *B*. Move along the path the number of spaces indicated on the space you land on. To finish, you must land on a space marked *B* with an exact count. You cannot enter a space more than once, and you must move to a space with a number. Landing on a blank is a "dead end."

Bingo Maze

Five of the answers to the following problems produce BINGO in the game board below. This means that five of the answers will line up horizontally, vertically, or diagonally. Some of the other answers will also be found on the board. Find the five problems.

a. $34 \times 56 - 18 =$

b. $512 + 349 - 146 =$

c. $2076 - 192 - 923 =$

d. $1715 \div 35 + 247 =$

e. $39 + 294 + 728 =$

f. $63 \times 27 - 235 =$

g. $22 \times 9 \times 24 =$

h. $288 \div 12 + 211 =$

i. $215 + 49 + 62 =$

j. $1000 - 210 - 69 =$

k. $144 \times 12 \div 36 =$

l. $6 \times 8 \times 3 \times 8 =$

m. $12 \times 12 \times 12 =$

n. $24 + 327 =$

o. $29,163 - 28,728 =$

p. $38 \times 19 =$

q. $2050 \div 25 =$

r. $2050 - 1902 + 24 =$

s. $214 + 823 - 661 =$

t. $35,650 \div 31 \div 25 =$

u. $326 + 295 =$

v. $1 \times 2 \times 3 \times 4 \times 5 \times 6 =$

w. $1301 - 499 - 106 =$

x. $214 + 562 - 129 =$

B	I	N	G	O
2146	326	351	621	722
721	2066	222	235	3095
4752	561	FREE	1728	46
191	715	529	172	1206
245	1886	826	696	376

Five problems that made a BINGO: ___ ___ ___ ___ ___

Collection Maze #1

Follow the lines from any star (✳) to another, passing through all the dollar signs ($). The path may never touch itself—not even at one point.

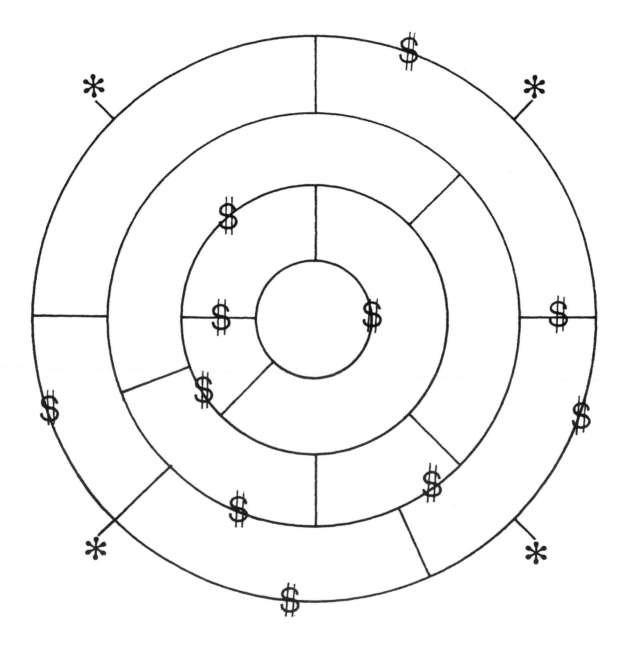

19   *Math Mazes*

Collection Maze #2

Follow the lines from any star (✳) to another, passing through all the dollar signs ($). The path may never touch itself—not even at one point.

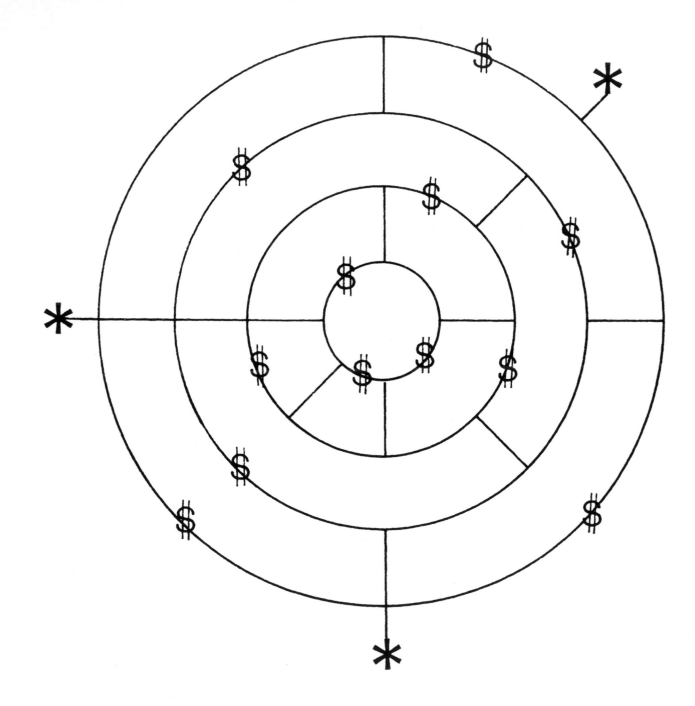

Fraction Maze

Move from the starting row to the finish row. However, you must always move to a smaller amount.

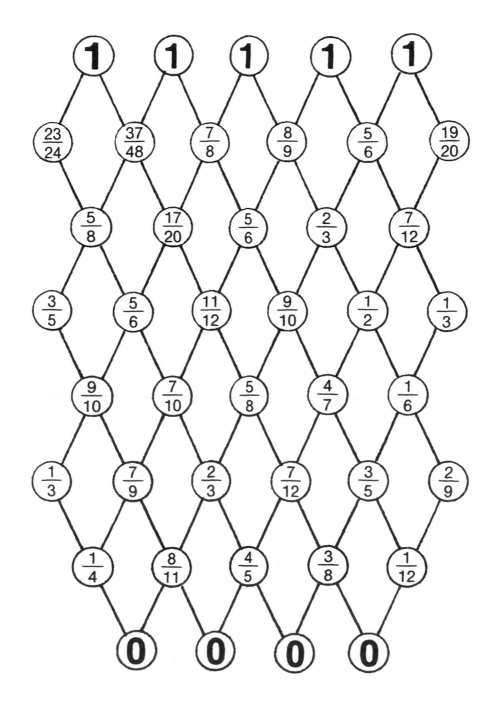

"Perfect Fit" Maze

The following 11 shapes will fit within the figure below. Use a pencil; you may have to erase and start again. It is best to begin at the starting point and draw towards the finish line.

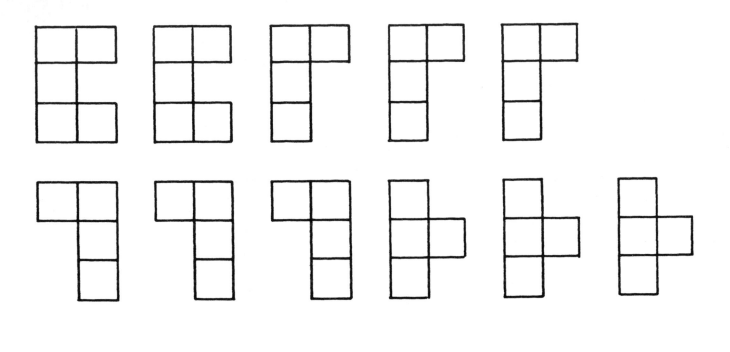

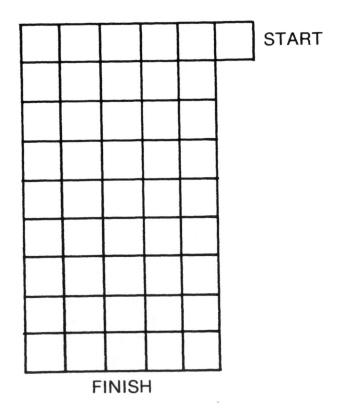

START

FINISH

Dollar Maze

Start and finish at the star following the connecting lines. The sum of the path should be $1. You must start and finish on the star without passing through it at any other time. Amounts may be used more than once.

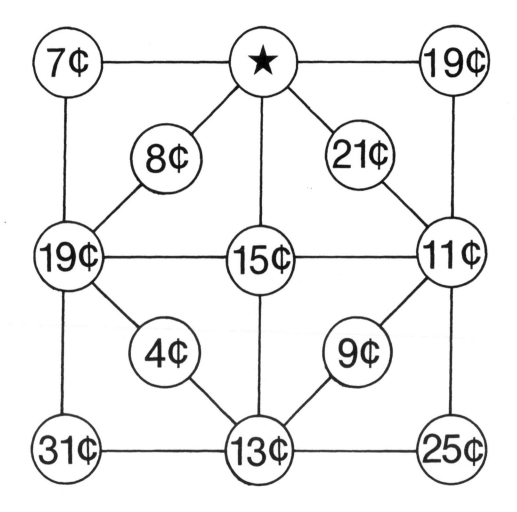

 Math Mazes

Magic Square Maze

Place two "8's," one "6," five "4's," two "3's," and four "2's" in the 14 squares below so the two rows and three columns will each equal 16.

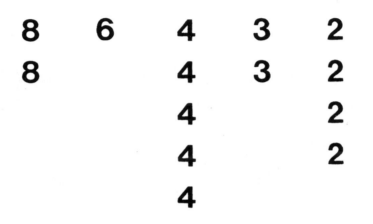

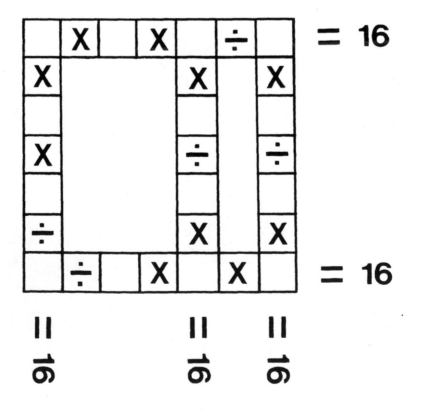